FUNTASTIC SKITS
FOR
CHILDREN'S
MINISTRY

Loveland, Colorado

Funtastic Skits for Children's Ministry
Copyright © 1993 Group Publishing, Inc.

CREDITS:
Edited by Beth Rowland
Interior designed by Dori Walker
Cover designed by Liz Howe
Cover illustrated by Nancy Tobin

Library of Congress Cataloging-in-Publication Data
   Funtastic skits for children's ministry / [edited by Beth Rowland].
       p.   cm.
     ISBN 1-55945-162-9
     1. Drama in Christian education. 2. Christian drama, American. I. Rowland, Beth.
     BV1534.4.F86   1993
     246'.7—dc20   93-19620
                                       CIP

12 11 10 9 8 7 6 5 4   04 03 02 01 00 99 98 97 96
Printed in the United States of America.

CONTENTS

INTRODUCTION

TEACHING KIDS WITH DRAMA

by Linda Shepherd

Drama is a "funtastic" way to teach kids because kids have a tremendous appetite for adventure and challenge. Using interactive drama with kids will help them:

- grasp faith concepts,
- face tough issues,
- find spiritual truth,
- examine attitudes,
- learn to cooperate with others,
- gain self-confidence,
- defend their beliefs, and
- develop their relationships with God.

Exploring real-life situations through skits intrigues kids because they love to use their imaginations to solve problems.

Here's what some kids have said about the power of drama:

- "Watching the skit helped me understand why I needed Jesus in my life."
- "Pretending to be another character helped me understand others."
- "Acting gave me confidence. When I was acting, I couldn't goof up. If I did, it was my character and not me."

Drama Helps Kids Learn by Doing

It's been said that the easiest way to teach children the value of money is to borrow some from them. This concept can be applied when teaching children spiritual truths. No lesson is better learned than one from life itself.

That's why drama is so powerful. Drama is made up of *slices of life*. It allows children to explore concepts, feelings, and ideas in the safety of a pretend world. When kids are acting out skits, they learn about "real life" by imitating it.

Drama Can Help Kids Understand the Bible

When kids use skits to try on different characters and situations, they discover that God's truth and love apply to everyone. Skits also give kids a chance to rehearse Biblical truths so they'll know how to apply them to their own lives.

Drama Helps Kids Build Teamwork and Trust

Drama teaches kids that cooperation produces results. They'll discover that the team effort of acting is fun! They'll become closer to each other. They'll learn to support, help, and encourage each other.

Drama Affirms Kids

Drama gives kids opportunities to sparkle and inspire. Skits can help kids take leading roles, instead of getting lost in the crowd. Drama is a great way to help kids discover their talents as they learn and teach spiritual truth to their peers.

Drama gives kids positive attention. Some kids will do anything to get into the spotlight. Why not challenge their creative energy with skits? They'll learn that applause is more rewarding than scoldings.

TIPS THAT PRODUCE RESULTS

What to do if your kids are shy...

● Encourage everyone to participate. If a child feels shy, give him or her a behind-the-scenes option such as working with sound effects.

● Allow a shy actor to hold a prop such as a ball or a sign. Children feel safer when they can hide behind something.

● The fun warm-ups found in the next chapter are great tools to help kids get beyond stage fright.

What to do if kids don't read well...

● Talk about the script ahead of time, and then let the children say their lines in their own words.

● Find creative ways to let kids pantomime or use sound effects. Maybe some children could act their parts without words, or maybe they could play squeaky doors or barking dogs.

How to turn on the dramatic, yet stay in control...

● Wait! Don't speak until kids are quiet. Don't raise your voice to be heard over the clamor. Speak in a normal tone of voice. The kids will stop talking so they can hear you.

● Use a signal that means "It's time to pay attention." You could flash the lights on and off or clap your hands three times. Insist on quiet whenever your signal is sounded.

● Make contracts with children who need special attention. For example, ask, "Does being the cowboy interest you? I will agree to let you try this role, if you agree to cooperate."

● If a child is spoiling the skit for the class with inappropriate behavior, take him or her aside and explain the problem. Ask for the child's help in solving the problem.

How to pick actors...

● Remember, your goal is to get kids to learn. *What they learn is more important than a polished performance.* Don't be afraid to give everyone a chance for a part.

● To maintain order and avoid favoritism, give roles to the children who aren't screaming for parts. This ensures the group will stay in control and the shy kids will have a chance to participate.

● Don't force a child to perform; wait until he or she is ready. Give this child the option of watching the skit carefully. Be sure to include him or her in the discussion time.

How to get started...

● Introduce a scene by describing the action and the characters. Let everyone take turns reading different portions of the script aloud. Or, read the skit aloud to the children. You may want to give a brief overview of the questions the skit will raise.

How to finish...

● During the discussion time, reflect, rephrase, and summarize the children's responses. Don't forget, the audience plays a big part in the dramatic process as it perceives, responds to, and evaluates the staged action.

Setting the mood...

Creating a mood with costumes, sound effects, and lighting is optional with these skits because they're designed as teaching tools rather than as performance dramas. Yet, if time allows, costumes, sound effects, and lighting can add to the fun. Here are a few suggestions:

● Costumes—You may want a big box or a trunk that you and the children can contribute to with scarves, wigs, hats, and dress-up clothes. Yard sales, attics, and spring cleaning yield wonderful costumes and props.

Keep in mind that one of the best costumes kids can wear is *body language*. A child playing an old man may walk on unsteady legs or hold his aching back. A child playing a toddler may skip and wiggle, while a child playing a coach might chew gum, wave his arms a lot, or bounce a ball when he talks.

● Sound Effects—Great sound effects can be invented spontaneously by a child assigned to the task, or taped into a recorder. For example, kids can slap their thighs to make the sound of a horse running, hum and chug like the sound of an engine, or whine a "squeak" whenever a door is opened. Music is great, too. A live piano or taped theme music can create effective moods.

● Lighting—Dim the lights for a romantic or mysterious effect. Brighten the lights for day scenes. A couple of flashlights make a great low-budget spotlight. Experimenting with Christmas lights can be fun, too.

WARM-UPS

Warm-Ups

by Julianne Bruce

These activities will help your kids practice their acting skills. They'll also help kids become more comfortable with acting in class. Use these activities to get your kids warmed up and ready to act.

Watch the Birdie

This warm-up will help children think about what their faces and bodies are doing when they portray different emotions.

Form trios. Make sure each trio has enough space to move around. Have each trio choose one person to be the photographer. The other two will be models. Prepare a list of emotions. Here are some ideas:

- depressed
- exhausted
- angry
- excited
- frustrated
- suspicious
- lonely
- sleepy
- happy
- dreamy

As you call out an emotion, have the models assume several poses showing that emotion. Have the photographers give them pointers if the models are having trouble. Once you've called out all the emotions, have the kids in each group switch roles.

What's It Like?

Use this warm-up to help kids remember details to use when they act.

Ask the kids to sit in a circle. Give each person a sheet of paper and a pencil. Have each person think of an activity such as eating a sundae or brushing a horse. Then they should imagine that activity in as much detail as they can and write down everything they can think of. Have them think of sounds, emotions, physical sensations, and smells, as well as each specific action that is involved in doing the activity.

When the kids have had a chance to write down all the details, have them tell what their activities are and read their action lists. After each description is read, have the whole group pantomime it, using as many of the details from the list as possible.

Is That What I Meant?

This warm-up will teach kids that *how* things are said can cause the message to be perceived differently than the speaker intended.

Write several phrases, such as "Happy birthday," "I don't like you," and "I love you," on a large sheet of paper or on a chalkboard. Next to the phrases list emotions, such as giggly, weepy, and fearful. Form pairs and have partners practice saying the phrases to each other using the emotions you've listed. Tell the group to listen to how some of the phrases sound silly and how some of them sound right. Have them notice that the meaning of what they say can get twisted by their tone of voice.

What If . . .

Prepare a list of "What if . . ." questions that require both a vocal and physical response. Here are some sample questions:

What if . . .
● there was a tornado here at church?
● you got to be the principal and make new rules?
● you grew to be 30 feet tall?
● you were about to parachute from an airplane for the first time?
● you found a box of kittens on your porch?
● you saw a robbery?

Ask each person one of the questions. The kids respond by acting out what they'd do. Their answers can be brief or they can be short scenes.

Story Time

This warm-up will help kids learn how to improvise actions for a familiar story.

Find several stories, nursery rhymes, or poems that the group would be familiar with, such as "Goldilocks and the Three Bears" or "The Itsy, Bitsy Spider." Choose one person to be the reader and choose others to represent the characters in the story or poem. Have the reader read the piece aloud while the characters act out the story.

Choose a new reader for each story or poem.

It's Recess!

Use masking tape to mark off an area in the room to represent the boundaries of a playground. Make sure there's nothing inside the area. On large sheets of paper, write down different pieces of playground equipment, such as swings, monkey bars, slides, and a merry-go-round. Tape these pieces of paper to the floor within the boundaries. Leave enough room inside the area for the kids to move around.

Tell the kids that they've all turned into 5-year-olds and it's time for kindergarten recess. Show them the playground and tell them that they may play on anything in the playground. Have the kids "play" on the different pieces of equipment as small children would.

After a few minutes, end the warm-up and have the kids sit in a circle. Ask them to talk about playing like a small child again. Find out which pieces of equipment were easiest to mime. Ask them if they liked being little kids again or if they like being older.

May I Help You?

This warm-up will teach children how to interact as characters with other characters. It will also help them recall details about people and strengthen their improvisational skills.

In advance, prepare slips of paper with careers written on them. The jobs should be nongender-specific and should allow plenty of opportunity for action. Here are some ideas:

- police officer
- professional wrestler
- garbage collector
- librarian
- doctor
- sales person
- lawyer
- teacher
- singer

Have each participant choose a slip of paper. Give kids a few moments to think of all of the different actions and types of language associated with their careers.

Choose two volunteers to start the exercise. Set the scene for them: They accidentally run into each other in the park. Each character must react to the other character using motions and phrases that someone in their career might use.

There doesn't have to be any preliminary action to the scene. For instance, the police officer might start by saying, "You're under arrest!" The scene doesn't necessarily have to make sense either. The librarian can respond to the police officer by saying, "Shhh! You must be quiet."

As the scene slows down, choose a person with another career to replace one of the actors, switching until everyone has had a turn.

A Walk in the Great Outdoors

This active warm-up will help kids explore movement.

Get kids on their feet and make sure they have plenty of room to move. Do a gentle warm-up by leading kids in some stretches to help them feel how their muscles work.

Tell the kids that they're going to use the space around them to explore the world. There are many types of terrain to cover. As they make their way through each one, remind them to make their actions as realistic as possible. For example, they can't run quickly in mud, and they must use their entire bodies to make their way through deep water.

As you lead the exploration, here are some types of terrain to cover:

- a field with tall grass
- a muddy riverbank
- a dry, rocky riverbed
- a sloping hill with trees
- a steep mountain trail
- a hot, sandy beach
- a fast-flowing river

As you travel, have the kids call out details that they "notice" such as snake holes or slippery rocks. Encourage everyone to include these in the trip.

Once the exploration is over, have the kids sit down on a "grassy slope" and talk about the trip. Ask which terrain was the hardest to get through and what kind of area they liked best.

Going Up?

Mark off a square area on the floor that's large enough to accommodate the entire group. This will serve as the perimeter of your acting space.

Have the participants choose a character for themselves, such as a shopper, a construction worker, or a business person. They must react to everything that happens as that character would. Have the kids stand inside the acting area. Then give them the scenario and introduce the problem.

Try these scenarios:

- an earthquake hits in a restaurant
- a music star shows up in a line for concert tickets
- fire sprinklers turn on in a shopping mall
- a mouse gets loose in an elevator that's stuck between floors

Here's an example of how to set up this warm-up using the last scenario listed:

When the kids get on the elevator, tell them to act as people act on elevators; for example, turning to face the doors, pressing buttons, and watching the floors go by. Once everyone is inside, tell them that the elevator has gotten stuck between floors. Once they start interacting about that problem, tell them there's a mouse loose on the elevator. What will they do? Where is the mouse going? Is it around their feet? Did it run into a shopping bag? When someone solves the problem or when things get too excited, tell the kids the elevator is running again and that they can now exit.

On the Bus

This warm-up will help kids work together to create the atmosphere of a bus ride.

Choose one volunteer to be the bus driver. The rest of the group should sit in two rows behind the driver, as if they were sitting on the bus. The driver leads the warm-up by calling out directions such as "right turn," "here comes a red light," or "bus stop #30." The rest of the group will follow the driver's lead with actions such as swaying sideways or coming to an abrupt halt.

Kids can interact further by simulating the actions of bus riders such as pulling the bell cord to signal the driver to stop, getting off and on the bus, or putting change in a slot. Also encourage them to mimic the sounds of a bus or make small talk with other passengers.

Planting a Feeling

Teach group members to express different emotions while doing another activity. This will help them to stay in character when they incorporate actions into their scenes.

Have kids form pairs and have partners number off 1 and 2. Have partner 1 mime the planting of a garden; for example, raking, watering, and planting. Have partner 2 come up with three emotions such as excited, sad, and angry. Partner 1 must work in the garden with whatever attitude partner 2 chooses. Partner 2 can change the emotion by calling out a new emotion. Once partner 1 has had the chance to act out each of the three emotions, have the pairs switch roles, and have partner 1 come up with three different emotions.

Zoo Escape

This warm-up will help the group learn to pay attention to other people's characters and actions in relation to their own while they're acting in a scene.

On slips of paper, write different animals that are found in a zoo. Let each person in the group choose one slip. Tell the kids that all of the cages at the zoo have accidentally been left open and all of the animals are loose.

As the members of the group act out their own animals, they must also react to the other animals they encounter. For example, if a lion comes across a monkey, the lion might roar, scaring the monkey away. Have the kids climb over and under tables and chairs to heighten their sense of becoming animals.

SKITS

'TIL DEATH DO US PART

Topic: Ruth

by Julianne Bruce

The Scene: On the road to Judah

Characters:

NAOMI (the mother-in-law)
RUTH (the first daughter-in-law)
ORPAH (the second daughter-in-law)

NAOMI   *(Stops walking and looks at the girls)* My dear daughters-in-law, you've come a long way. Thanks for looking out for me, but you really should be heading back. After all, it's still a long way to Bethlehem.

RUTH   Go back? We're not going back. Why do you think we brought all this luggage? We're going with you.

ORPAH   Yeah, and we sure didn't come all this way because it's National Health and Fitness Week.

NAOMI   Very funny, girls, but I mean it. You've been good to me, looking after me since my husband's death. But now that both of your husbands have died, you should get on with your lives. Go back to your own families. Go home to your mothers where you'll be more comfortable.

ORPAH   But you're a much better cook than my mom! I think I'll go with you.

NAOMI   What about you, Ruth?

RUTH   My parents' house is really crowded right now. With the famine and everything, all of my brothers and sisters have moved back with all their kids. My father practically has a whole zoo with all the sheep and the oxen, and the dogs, and then there's...

NAOMI   You girls are too much! Please, don't keep following me. Go now, and may God bless you both.

RUTH   No. We mean it, Naomi. We're not going to go back. We're walking all the way to Bethlehem with you.

NAOMI   Why won't you do what I tell you? Go back to Moab and get settled with another husband.

ORPAH   But I don't have another husband!

RUTH   Please, Naomi, let us go with you. It's what we really want.

NAOMI   Quit arguing with me, girls. Go! I'm not taking you with me. *(Starts to walk away.)*

RUTH   But Naomi! *(Falls to her knees crying.)*

ORPAH   *(Starts crying, too)* Please! Please! Please!

NAOMI   *(Turns to them)* Why do you want to come with me? Do you think I'm going to have more sons so you'll have someone else to marry? Do you think I'm going to find another husband at my age?

RUTH   You're not so old. I saw that innkeeper at the last hotel smiling at you.

NAOMI   Now, stop that, Ruth. *(Sighs and shakes her head)* Look—it's not that I don't want your company. I love you both. But look at my life. God's hand is against me. I've lost my husband and both my sons. Terrible things just keep happening. Who knows what'll happen next!

ORPAH   I hadn't thought of that. No offense, but maybe I'll just be heading home.

NAOMI   Good girl, Orpah. *(Hugs her)* Go home and be safe. *(Orpah exits.)* And you too, Ruth. Go back with her.

RUTH   I told you already. I'm going with you. I really mean it. I want to go where you go. I want to eat where you eat. I want to pray where you pray! *(Getting overly dramatic)* I want to sing where you sing! I want to sneeze where you sneeze! Nothing in the world can ever tear me away from you! Hey, if you're ever in a jam, here I am. Death itself won't come between us! If you should...

NAOMI   OK, OK! You win. You can go with me. But it's been a hard life and it doesn't look like it's going to get much better.

RUTH   I don't mind. You're my family, and I want to be there for you.

NAOMI   Thanks, Ruth. You know, I've got this funny feeling you may have a big future in Bethlehem.

DISCUSSION STARTERS

1. Read Proverbs 17:17. Have you ever had a friend be especially loyal to you, even when things were difficult?

2. Why is it harder to be a good friend when someone is having problems?

3. What makes one person feel loyal to another?

4. What can you do to be a friend to God?

A QUEEN TO SAVE THE DAY

Topic: Esther

by Julianne Bruce

The Scene: The palace of King Xerxes

Characters:

QUEEN ESTHER (a beautiful and intelligent woman)
MORDECAI (Esther's cousin)
KING XERXES (a nice but befuddled man)
HAMAN (one of Xerxes' top officials, who thinks a lot of himself)

(The actions and voices should be exaggerated for comic effect.)

ESTHER   *(Dances happily on stage)* How wonderful the Lord is! I am the most blessed woman in the world! Of all the girls in all the land, the king picked me to be his queen. All those lotions and perfumes and all that beauty pageant training finally paid off. Life couldn't be more perfect!

MORDECAI   *(Runs on stage and is out of breath)* Esther! Esther! I need your help!

ESTHER   Why Cousin Mordecai! Whatever could the problem be? Just when I was thinking how wonderful life is, you come running in here like something's wrong.

MORDECAI   Something *is* wrong! There's a plot against our people! Haman, the king's official, plans to persuade your husband, the king, to kill all the Jews. You must go tell the king and beg his mercy.

ESTHER   Oh my! This is just terrible! Terrible! You know I'd really love to help you, Cousin. Truly I would. But there's just one problem. The king hasn't asked to see me in ages. I don't know if he's angry with me or if he's forgotten me. Now if I just go rushing in there, he could kill me just for bothering him.

MORDECAI   If you wait until he calls you, it could be too late. You're a Jew, Esther. The order to kill us all includes you.

ESTHER   Oh. Well, put like that, I don't have much to lose, do I?

MORDECAI   Nope.

ESTHER   OK, then I guess I just better get this nasty little task over with just as soon as I can. But you have to get everyone to pray for me. And I don't mean a quick little "bless her and keep her" prayer. I mean a great big "this is it or we're all coming home" kind of prayer that lasts for days and days. Got it?

MORDECAI   Anything you say. *(He exits.)*

(Esther sits down on the floor as though at a banquet table. Xerxes and Haman join her.)

HAMAN   You know, Queenie, I knew that once you and the king here spent an evening with me, you'd be dying to have me back. We're not having leftovers are we?

ESTHER   Why, Haman, that's not how we do things here in Persia.

XERXES   Esther, you know I'm pleased to see you again. Last night's dinner was excellent, and you were lovely. *(To Haman)* Isn't she just the most beautiful creature you ever saw? *(To Esther)* But, I'm a little confused. Why is it you wanted to have dinner with us again? You know I'll give you whatever you want—up to half my kingdom.

ESTHER   Well, King, there's just one little tiny thing that I have my heart set on. Since you did say up to half your kingdom, it'd be just lovely if your gift could be my life and the lives of my people.

XERXES   What? I don't understand. Haman, what did she ask me for?

ESTHER   You see, King, my people are the Jews, and since Haman had you sign that order to get rid of all of us, I was sort of hoping that, if it wouldn't be too much trouble, maybe you wouldn't kill us?

XERXES (*Horrified*) I signed an order to kill my own queen? When did I . . .

(*Haman tries to sneak away.*)

XERXES Haman, you lowdown, sneaky . . .

HAMAN Well, they were such a pain, Your Majesty. Especially that Mordecai. He set such a bad example. You know he wouldn't bow down to me. And it made me look bad. I mean really!

XERXES Haman, you asked me to get rid of a bad man. Well, I'm getting rid of one now. Get out of my sight!

DISCUSSION STARTERS

1. Read Esther 2:2-13. Esther spent a lot of time making herself beautiful for the king. How important is it to spend time on our outward appearance?

2. What qualities did Esther have that make her a good example for us?

3. Is it easier to recognize others' good character or their appearance? Explain. What can you do to find out about and encourage the good qualities others have?

THE NINEVITE EVENING NEWS

Topic: Jonah

by Rick Lawrence

The Scene: A television news studio

Characters:

ANNOUNCER	**REPORTER**
NEWSCASTER	**JONAH**

Props: A desk, a chair, and a microphone

(To begin, have all the kids who weren't assigned a role play tag on stage. There's a desk and a chair center stage, facing the audience. After a few seconds, Announcer and Newscaster walk to center stage. Newscaster sits behind the desk. Announcer stands in front of the desk. As soon as Announcer speaks, the kids playing tag freeze.)

ANNOUNCER   We interrupt our regularly scheduled game for this special report from the Ninevite *(say this Ni-nah-vite)* Evening News. *(Kids playing tag hurry off the stage. Announcer follows them off. Reporter and Jonah enter and stand with their backs to the audience. Reporter should carry a microphone.)*

NEWSCASTER   *(In a news-anchor voice)* Good evening. Here's what's happening. Just hours ago, a man calling himself Jonah, Prophet of God, started a near riot in the downtown area. Witnesses report they hear this man screaming—quote— After 40 days, Nineveh will be destroyed—end quote. Apparently, the king and all the people have taken this man seriously. The king has ordered city residents to publicly show how sorry they are for the wrong things they've done. We go to our top reporter for a live report.

REPORTER	*(Turns, holding microphone, to face the audience along with Jonah)* I'm standing here on the city streets with the man who calls himself Jonah, Prophet of God. Today this man has turned our city upside down. In response to Jonah's message of doom and gloom, the people have put on rough clothing and have vowed not to eat. Jonah, tell me how all this got started. *(Points microphone to Jonah.)*
JONAH	Well, I'll tell you. The last few days haven't been all that great for me. First, God told me to come to this rotten, old city and tell you all how rotten you've all been. Well, that didn't sound all that fun to me, so I hopped aboard a ship going the other way. Boy, was that a bad move!
REPORTER	Why is that?
JONAH	Well, once we got out to sea, God started this big storm that almost tore apart our ship. When the other sailors found out that I was running away from God, well, they just up and chucked me overboard. That's when a big, old fish came along and swallowed me up.
REPORTER	Excuse me? I must've heard you wrong. I thought you said a fish came and swallowed you.
JONAH	That's right. Just take a whiff of my shirt. *(Reporter sniffs shirt, then makes a sick face.)* Smells just like the inside of a fish, right? Well, I'll tell you. It's not every day I'm sittin' in a fish's belly. Kinda makes you think a little. I was wrong to try to run away from God, and I told him so. Next think I know *(pantomimes coughing up something)* I'm outta there. That's how I ended up here in Nineveh.
REPORTER	That's quite a story, Jonah. I've got to say I probably wouldn't have believed it myself if I hadn't smelled . . . I mean heard it myself. That's it from here. Back to you.
NEWSCASTER	Thank you. Remember to tune in here for the latest developments in this story.
ANNOUNCER	*(Enters and stands in front of the desk)* We now return you to our regularly scheduled game. *(Kids playing tag rush back onto stage and start playing again.)*

DISCUSSION STARTERS

1. If you had been Jonah and God told you to go to a big city and tell the people there how bad they were, what would you have done?

2. When you know you're supposed to do something and you don't do it, how do you feel? What does it take to change your mind?

3. When you know you're supposed to do something and you do it, how do you feel?

4. Read in Jonah 2:1-10 what Jonah said to God when he was in the fish's belly. What would you have said to God if you were Jonah?

THE DINNER GUEST

Topic: Mary and Martha

by Julianne Bruce

The Scene: Mary and Martha are preparing a meal for Jesus

Characters:

MARY
MARTHA
JESUS

(Mary and Martha pantomime fixing dinner for Jesus.)

MARY	I'm so excited that the Lord's coming to our house for dinner! Isn't it just the most amazing thing? Isn't it just too unbelievable?
MARTHA	It's unbelievable all right. Look how much we've got to do. If you don't stop jabbering at me, we'll never be ready. Have you checked the bread? Did you fold the napkins? Stir the sauce again. Move it, Mary! Will you quit daydreaming?
MARY	Dreaming? Oh yes, it is a dream come true! Imagine, Jesus choosing our home.
MARTHA	Imagine Jesus slipping in that soup you just spilled. Will you pay attention to what you're doing?
MARY	It's not every day that Jesus stops by for dinner. I hope none of the neighbors are burning with envy!
MARTHA	Burning! What's burning? The bread? Is it the bread? I thought I told you to check the bread! Are you listening?
MARY	I love listening to Jesus. Maybe he'll tell us a parable. That's what I'd love to hear.

MARTHA	Someone knocked. He's here. Don't just stand there! Go let him in!
MARY	Shouldn't I check the bread first?
MARTHA	Go!
MARY	*(Runs to answer the door)* Come in. Please sit down. I'm so glad you're here.
	(Martha comes into the room.)
JESUS	Thank you. I hope you didn't go to a lot of trouble.
MARY	Well, Martha's been going out of her mind...
MARTHA	*(Puts her hand over Mary's mouth)* What my sister means is that I hoped you wouldn't mind if dinner takes a few more minutes. Come on, Mary. *(Yanks her into the kitchen.)*
MARY	*(Turns right back around)* I was just telling Martha how excited I was that you're here, Lord. I heard you speaking in Jerusalem the other day.
JESUS	And what did you think? Please, sit.
MARY	*(Sits at his feet)* Well, actually, I had some questions...
MARTHA	*(Enters)* Yes, questions. Like how we're supposed to serve the Prince of Peace burned bread? Or how I'm supposed to finish the meat, cook the vegetables, run to the well for more water, and get out the good dishes all at the same time? Will you *please* tell my sister to get back to work?
JESUS	Martha, calm down. It's not the food that's important ...
MARTHA	Yes, but ...
JESUS	It's our time together that ...
MARTHA	I know, but ...
JESUS	So you should follow your sister's example and...
MARTHA	But ...

JESUS	Martha!
MARTHA	Yes?
JESUS	We have to make a lot of choices in life. Mary made the best choice. Come sit down. Let's talk.
MARTHA	*(Sits next to Mary)* OK, Lord, but life with Mary has never been easy.

DISCUSSION STARTERS

1. What things in your life are really important, and what things just seem important?

2. How do you decide whether something should have priority in your life?

3. How can you tell when something that has low priority is taking too much of your time or energy?

4. According to the story of Mary and Martha in Luke 10:38-42, what should be the most important thing in your life?

LAZARUS, COME FORTH!

Topic: Jesus Raises Lazarus

by Rich Melheim

The Scene: Jesus raises Lazarus from the dead.

Characters:

MARY **JESUS**

MARTHA **NARRATOR**

LAZARUS

Props:

Signs that say "weep," "wail," "dead," "applause," and "Lazarus, come forth!" You'll also need a roll of toilet paper. Roll up Lazarus in the toilet paper but make sure he can still walk and see.

NARRATOR   I'd like to introduce you to Jesus, his friend Lazarus, and Laz's sisters, Mary and Martha. I'll be counting on the rest of you to provide the sound effects that are written on these signs. *(Holds up signs)* Ready? Here goes: It was four days since Lazarus had died. Mary, Martha, and the crowd were weeping! *(Holds "weep" sign.)*

MARY, MARTHA, AUDIENCE   Weep! Weep!

NARRATOR   The crowd was wailing. *(Holds "wail" sign.)*

MARY, MARTHA, AUDIENCE   Wail! Wail!

NARRATOR   Lazarus was... *(Holds "dead" sign.)*

MARY, MARTHA, AUDIENCE	Dead!
LAZARUS	Aaaaarrrggghhh! *(Lazarus enters melodramatically, falls on the floor near Mary and Martha, flails about, and is finally still.)*
NARRATOR	The word finally got to Jesus. *(Jesus enters on the other side of the stage from Mary, Martha, and Lazarus. Narrator hands Jesus the "dead" sign.)*
JESUS	Dead? I'll go to him now. *(Jesus walks over to Mary, Martha, and Lazarus.)*
MARY, MARTHA	Lord, if you'd only been here, our brother wouldn't have died.
NARRATOR	And Jesus said:
JESUS	Your brother will rise and live again! I am the resurrection and the life. People who believe in me will live even if they die.
NARRATOR	Then Jesus stepped over to the tomb and said: *(Holds the "Lazarus, come forth!" sign.)*
JESUS, AUDIENCE	Lazarus, come forth!
NARRATOR	And Lazarus did. *(Narrator holds the "applause" sign. Lazarus jerks once, twice, and sits up.)*
MARY, MARTHA, AUDIENCE	*(Applaud)*
NARRATOR	And the moral of this story is:
LAZARUS	*(Rips the paper off his face and body. Then holds Jesus' hand up like a victorious prize fighter and lifts the "applause" sign)* Jesus has the power over death!

DISCUSSION STARTERS

1. Why are people so scared of dying? Why does God let people die?

2. Read 1 Corinthians 15:35-58. According to this passage, what can you look forward to? Is it wrong to be sad when someone dies? Why or why not?

3. Describe what you think heaven will be like.

THE CRAZY BOAT RIDE

Topic: Jesus Calms a Storm

by Julianne Bruce

The Scene: Luke recounts the story of Jesus calming the storm, as the disciples act it out with him.

Characters:

LUKE (the narrator)
JESUS
11 DISCIPLES (These characters can be of either gender. If your class is small, use fewer disciples.)
STORM (Have the audience make storm noises when Luke starts talking about the storm.)

LUKE   Have I got a story to tell you! You'll never believe it. I wouldn't believe it, except I was there. One day, Jesus wanted to go to the other side of Lake Galilee. Now a lot of us disciples had been fishermen before we joined up with Jesus, so we knew there was a killer storm coming when we saw the clouds building up. The lake was big and that storm could hit before we got across. But Jesus asked, so what could we say? He always seemed to know what he was doing, so we got in the boat.

(Luke, the disciples, and Jesus get into the boat. Everyone takes part in sailing the boat. Some can work the sails while others raise the anchor. All this continues while Luke talks. Jesus lies down and goes to sleep.)

LUKE   Now Jesus had been working hard to spread the good news, and he was tired. Nobody could blame him when he fell asleep. But that storm did come, and boy was it a bad one! We got tossed around and the waves were filling the boat with water.

(Audience makes storm noises. Disciples mimic being tossed

around, yelling, holding onto each other and bailing water.)

LUKE   We thought we'd never make it. And Jesus just kept sleeping!

(Disciples panic, yelling things like "We're gonna die!" "Someone help us!" and "What are we gonna do?")

LUKE   Then I had an idea. We should wake Jesus up. He'd know what to do. So we woke him up.

(Disciples crowd around Jesus, shaking him and asking for help.)

LUKE   *This* is the part you'll never believe.

JESUS   *(Gets up and raises his hands in the air)* Winds, be still. Sea, be calm. In my name, this storm will stop.

(Disciples quit rocking and falling, look around in wonder, and begin to smile.)

LUKE   Isn't that the most incredible thing you ever saw? We sure couldn't believe it. But then something even worse than the storm happened.

JESUS   *(Turns to disciples)* Where is your faith? Did you think I'd let you all die? I thought you knew me better than that. You all have a lot to learn.

LUKE   We felt really bad for doubting him. After all, we knew he was amazing. We'd seen lots of other miracles. But this time he even made the wind and the water obey him. We sure did have a lot to learn.

DISCUSSION STARTERS

1. Read Mark 4:35-41. How do you think you would've felt if you had been one of the disciples in the boat?

2. Why did Jesus tell the disciples that they had a lot to learn?

3. Was there ever a time when you didn't trust God to protect you? When has God protected you?

PLANTING FOR A HARVEST

Topic: The Sower and the Seed

by Julianne Bruce

The Scene: A farmer plants his seeds.

Characters:

NARRATOR	**SECOND SEEDS**
FARMER	**THIRD SEEDS**
FIRST SEEDS	**FOURTH SEEDS**

NARRATOR   Once upon a time, there was a farmer who went out to plant his seeds.

FARMER   What a great day to plant my seeds. *(He tosses seeds on the ground.)*

FIRST SEEDS   *(Tumbles on the ground where the farmer indicated.)*

NARRATOR   But, he wasn't such a smart farmer . . .

FARMER   Hey!

NARRATOR   Just look where you threw your seeds.

FARMER   I guess I shouldn't have thrown them on the path. Do you think they'll grow there?

NARRATOR   Nope. They'll just lie there until the birds come and eat them.

FIRST SEEDS   Birds? I'm going to get eaten by birds? No way! I'm outta here! *(Exits.)*

FARMER   Hmm. That didn't work too well. Maybe I'll toss some over here and over here. *(Tosses seeds in two different spots.)*

SECOND SEEDS	*(Tumbles to the ground in one spot that the farmer indicated.)*
THIRD SEEDS	*Tumbles to the ground in the other spot that the farmer indicated.)*
FARMER	How's that? Do I know how to farm or what?
NARRATOR	Or what. Sorry, you did it wrong again.
FARMER	But there's dirt over there! *(Points to Second Seeds.)*
NARRATOR	But it's only shallow soil. Those seeds can't take root.
SECOND SEEDS	*(Claws at ground)* Nice job, farmer. There's nothing under this soil but rock.
NARRATOR	When the sun shines on those seeds, they'll dry up and wither away.
SECOND SEEDS	Water, water! *(Mimics dying of thirst and falls over. Exits.)*
FARMER	So what's wrong with over here? *(Points to Third Seeds.)*
NARRATOR	That's where the thorns are. Those seeds can't survive there, either.
THIRD SEEDS	*(Mimics being pricked by thorns.)* Ouch! Ouch! I'm a plant, not Swiss cheese! Ouch! Just forget it! *(Exits.)*
FARMER	I give up! Where am I supposed to plant the seeds?
NARRATOR	Look for a place where your seeds can put down deep roots and where there aren't other plants that will choke them out.
FARMER	*(Searches the ground, tests the soil until he finds a place)* I've got it! Right here. *(He throws the seeds down.)*
FOURTH SEEDS	*(Tumbles to the ground in the spot where the farmer indicated.)*
FARMER	*(Looks at Narrator)* Right?
FOURTH SEEDS	*(Stretches out as though sunbathing.)* What a great spot. Waiter? I'll have a large water with a twist of fertilizer, please.

NARRATOR   Exactly. Now your seeds will grow, and you'll have a big harvest.

FARMER   Cool!

NARRATOR   You know, it works the same way when people hear God's Word. If people hear God's Word, understand it, make it a part of themselves, and focus only on God, then they'll grow like the seeds in the good soil.

FARMER   Wow! And to think it all started with spring planting. You know, with your talent for words and my ability to raise a crop, we have the beginning of a beautiful friendship here. (*They exit.*)

DISCUSSION STARTERS

1. Read Psalm 1. What can you do to put down deep roots in good soil?

2. What kinds of things can choke out your relationship with God?

3. Read Matthew 13:23. What kind of crops is Jesus talking about?

4. What are some ways you can tell you're growing in your relationship with God?

WHAT'S BEHIND DOOR #2?

Topic: The Prodigal Son

by Rick Lawrence

The Scene: The *Let's Make a Deal* game show.

Characters:

MONTY HALL	**CAROL**	**THREE PIGS**
PRODIGAL SON	**FATHER**	

Props: A microphone, a podium, newsprint, a sign that says "Ooooh, aaaah!" and a sign that says "Bleckkk, gross!"

(Write "Door #1" on one sheet of newsprint and "Door #2" on another sheet of newsprint. Have Father stand center stage and hide behind the Door #1 sign. Have the three pigs kneel single file with the Door #2 sign in front of them. Carol stands off to one side holding the other two signs. Monty Hall enters, runs to the podium, and picks up the microphone. Prodigal son is seated in the audience.)

MONTY HALL   Welcome to *Let's Make a Deal!* I'm Monty Hall, and I'm here to make you a deal! Now, who'll be my first contestant?

PRODIGAL SON   *(Waving hands wildly)* Me! Me! Pick me!

MONTY HALL   All right, young man. Right, you in the front row. Come on up. Let's give him a big hand. *(Applause.)* OK, I'll tell you what: I'll trade you whatever you have in your pocket for what's behind Door #1. What do you say?

PRODIGAL SON   Oh wow! Are you kidding? All I've got is this little ball of lint. You can have it!

MONTY HALL	And you can have the fabulous prize behind Door #1. Carol, show him what he's won!
CAROL	*(Removes Door #1 newsprint and holds up "Ooooh, aaaah!" sign)* That's right! You've just won your very own father! Let's look at what he has to offer. First, he's a very generous man who'll give you everything you need for a good life. Second, he promises to love you like no father ever loved his son. And third, he'll leave you one half of all his property as your inheritance!
MONTY HALL	Oh my! What an incredible prize. But I'll tell you what. How'd you like to trade your father and your inheritance for what's behind Door #2?
PRODIGAL SON	Hey, this is bogus! Whatever's behind Door #2 has gotta be better than what I've got! Monty, you've got yourself a deal!
MONTY HALL	OK! Carol, show him what he's traded for!
CAROL	You bet, Monty! *(Pulls away Door #2 newsprint from the pigs. The pigs should immediately start making snorting noises. Carol holds up the "Bleckkk, gross!" sign.)* That's right! You've just traded in your incredible father and your inheritance for a bunch of pigs! They'll be your constant companions for the rest of your life! You'll even get to share their food! Come on up and take 'em off our hands!
PRODIGAL SON	Oh no! I can't believe I did that! I blew it big time! I'm stuck with these pigs for the rest of my life. Please, please let me trade back.
MONTY HALL	Oh no, I'm sorry. All trades are final. You'll just have to get used to eating slop instead of cereal in the morning!
PRODIGAL SON	*(Sadly)* Maybe I'll go back to my father even if I can't trade these pigs back.
FATHER	Wait a minute—did you just say you'd like to come back to me?
MONTY HALL	Yes, but it doesn't matter now.

FATHER   It matters to me, son! Come on back!

PRODIGAL   *(Embarrassed)* You mean, you're not mad at me or anything?
SON

FATHER   Are you kidding? I'm just glad you decided to come back! It's
               party time! Monty, Carol, you can come to the party, too.
               (Pauses) But not the pigs. *(Everyone exits but the pigs.)*

DISCUSSION STARTERS

1. Read Ephesians 4:32. Think of a time you needed forgiveness from someone—how did you feel? How did you feel when the person forgave you?
How did you feel when the person didn't forgive you?

2. How is the father in the skit like God? How is the prodigal son in this story
like you? Can you do anything so bad that God would never forgive you?
Why or why not?

3. Why do you think Jesus decided to tell this story to the people? How does
this story change the way you think about God?

PEANUT BUTTER PUSHERS

Topic: Drugs

by Mike Nappa

The Scene: A schoolyard.
Characters:

PAULY PUSHER   **REX**   **TINA**
JODY   **KEVIN**

Props: A jar of chunky peanut butter and two spoons.

(Pauly Pusher, Rex, and Jody are standing center stage acting cool. Kevin and Tina enter from stage left. If you prefer a smaller cast, combine the roles of Kevin and Tina, and Rex and Jody.)

PAULY PUSHER	*(To Kevin and Tina)* Psst! Hey you guys. C'mere.
TINA	*(As she and Kevin walk over to Pauly)* What do you want, Pauly?
PAULY PUSHER	I've got something for ya. Something really good. Look! *(He pulls the jar of peanut butter from under his shirt.)*
KEVIN	Peanut butter! That stuff will rot your brains. No wonder you don't have anything better to do than hang around the schoolyard all day. Forget it—we don't want any.
REX	*(Laughing)* He's chicken! What a loser!
PAULY PUSHER	*(To Tina)* Hey, why don't you ditch this loser and come to a peanut butter party with me and my friends?
TINA	No thanks, Pauly. Peanut butter messes with your mind and makes you talk funny.

PAULY PUSHER	*(Annoyed)* Shows how much you know. Watch this. *(He gives Rex and Jody each a large spoonful of peanut butter.)* Show 'em, gang.
REX, JODY	*(Each with a mouthful of peanut butter)* She sells seashells by the seashore. Rubber baby buggy bumpers. Pauly Pusher picked a peck of pickled peppers.
PAULY PUSHER	*(Thoughtfully)* Hey, maybe you're right. *(To Kevin and Tina)* Let's get outta here.

(Pauly hands the peanut butter jar and spoons to Rex and Jody, then exits stage right with Kevin and Tina. Rex and Jody shrug their shoulders and eat another spoonful of peanut butter before they exit.)

DISCUSSION STARTERS

1. How was this skit like or unlike the way people encourage drug use?

2. Why do people experiment with drugs? Read Proverbs 23:29-35. How does this picture of drug abuse compare to the image drug users present about drugs?

3. Read 1 Corinthians 6:19-20. How does this verse affect your attitude toward drugs? Explain.

Can You Top That?

Topic: Being a Child of God

by Mike Nappa

The Scene: A game show.

Characters

GAME SHOW HOST   **PLAYER #2**
PLAYER #1   **PLAYER #3**

Props: "Applause" cue card.

(Three players are seated center stage. Game Show Host stands to the left, holding the "Applause" cue card.)

HOST   *(With enthusiasm)* Good day, and welcome to "Can You Top That!" *(Flashes "Applause" cue card to audience)* As you all know, this is the game where people take turns trying to "out-brag" each other. Bragging is judged on a scale from 1 to l0, and the player with the best boast wins. The topic for today's brag-fest is "families." Well, what're we waiting for? Let's get on with "Can You Top That?" *(Flashes "Applause" cue card)* Player #1, go!

PLAYER #1   OK, well, let's see. My sister is so great ...

HOST, PLAYERS #2 AND #3   *(Shouting in unison)* How great is she?

PLAYER #1   My sister is so great she once climbed Mount Rushmore and "picked" Abe Lincoln's nose! *(Appeals to audience for applause.)*

HOST   Not bad, #1, not bad. Let's see what our judges say. On a scale of 1 to l0, your boast rates a 6.5! *(Flashes "Applause" cue card)* Player #2, can you top that?

PLAYER #2   Well, I'll sure try. My uncle is so great...

HOST, PLAYERS #1 AND #3   *(Shouting in unison)* How great is he?

PLAYER #2   My uncle is so great he once stuffed 37 snails in his mouth at the same time!

HOST   Whoa! Bet he felt sluggish after that. Let's see what our judges say. On a scale of 1 to 10, your boast rates a 7.9! *(Flashes "Applause" cue card)* Player #3, can you top that?

PLAYER #3   *(Stifling a yawn)* A member of my family is so great...

HOST, PLAYERS #1 AND #2   *(Shouting in unison)* How great is your family member?

PLAYER #3   Well, my family member is so great he once created the entire universe. You see, I'm a member of God's family, and God is the powerful creator of everything we see.

PLAYERS #1 AND #2   *(Mouths drop open. Then shaking heads, they shuffle offstage.)* Can't beat that one.

PLAYER #3   *(Happily)* Yes! Gets 'em every time.

HOST   Congratulations, #3, your boast scores a perfect 10! *(Flashes "Applause" cue card)* That's it for today, folks. Thanks for joining us once again for "Can You Top That?" *(Flashes "Applause" cue card.)*

Discussion Starters

1. Read John 1:12; Philippians 2:12-15; and 1 John 3:1-2. What are some characteristics of God you can brag about?

2. How would you define "being a child of God?" What benefits come with being a child of God? What responsibilities?

3. Why do you think God wants us to be his children? How do we become his children?

ABOUT THAT TREEHOUSE

Topic: Solving Problems

by Mike Nappa

The Scene: Friends are planning to build a treehouse.

Characters:

CARL
TYLER
JANE

(Carl and Jane are looking over imaginary blueprints as they discuss their plans for building a treehouse.)

CARL   OK, the way I see it, if we put the floor of the club treehouse on the fourth branch up to the right, we'll have a sturdy base and a great view of the high school football field as well.

JANE   No, no, no. We should put it on the third branch up on the left so we can have a clear look at the shopping center. That way we'll be the first to know if there's a sale on Rollerblades.

TYLER   *(Runs in, breathless)* Hold everything, troops. We've got problems, big problems. Johnnie says if we build our treehouse in this tree, it'll block his view of the drive-in theater. Johnnie and his friends are on their way over here to make us stop right now! Oh, I think I'm gonna be sick.

JANE   Uh-oh. Last time somebody blocked Johnnie's view, that person was found hanging upside down in the monkey cage at the zoo.

TYLER   Yeah, with chocolate-covered bananas stuffed in his ears. Oh, I think I'm gonna have a headache.

CARL   Just wait a minute. What are our options?

JANE   We could run away to France.

TYLER   We could all have heart attacks before he gets here.

CARL   Be serious. We have a right to build a treehouse if we want to.

TYLER   Are you gonna tell Johnnie that? Who do you think you are? God?

CARL   *(After a beat)* No, but God is a friend of mine. Excuse me a second. *(He kneels to pray. After a minute, he rises.)* OK, here I go. I'm gonna go have a talk with Johnnie. *(He exits.)*

TYLER   *(Shouting after Carl)* Wouldn't you rather splash lemon juice on a paper cut?

JANE   *(Sadly, with a hand over her heart)* Goodbye, Carl! It's been nice knowing you!

TYLER   How long before we hear the cries of torture?

JANE   Two minutes, max.

               (Tyler and Jane pause, cup their ears, and wait to hear the screams.)

JANE   Say, was that thunder?

TYLER   *(Nodding)* Yeah, I think so. *(Shrugs his shoulders and keeps listening.)*
               (After about 30 seconds, Carl re-enters, smiling.)

JANE   Carl! You're alive!

TYLER   *(Looking in Carl's ears)* And no bananas! *(To himself)* Too bad, being scared always makes me hungry. *(To Carl)* What happened?

CARL   Simple. I told Johnnie I'm not scared of him because I'm a Christian and God is protecting me. Just then, there was a huge clap of thunder. *(Shrugs his shoulders)* Johnnie and his pals got scared and ran away.

JANE,   Wow!
TYLER

CARL   So, anyway, I still think we should build the treehouse on the fourth branch. What do you guys think?

Discussion Starters

1. Read Nehemiah 4:1-15. How was this skit similar to the situation Nehemiah faced in this passage? How were Carl's and Nehemiah's responses to their problems similar or different?

2. How do you feel when you're in situations similar to these? What other types of problems do you face? How do you respond to those problems or situations?

3. How can God help you when you face a problem?

4. Do you ever feel like God doesn't care about your problems? Why? What do you do when God doesn't seem to help you solve a problem?

I Wanna Be...

Topic: Growing Up

by Mike Nappa

The Scene: Friends talking about the future.
Characters:

DUKE   **JESSICA**
KAREN   **NATHAN**

(Duke, Karen, Jessica, and Nathan are all sitting center stage.)

DUKE   What's there to think about? When I grow up, I wanna be one of those guys who pretends to be Elvis.

JESSICA   Do you even know any Elvis songs?

DUKE   *(Annoyed)* Of course I do. *(Stands to perform, sings)* Well, since my baby left me ... uh ... something, something, oh yeah ... uh, row, row, row your boat ... uh ... *(Sits)* OK, maybe I need a little practice.

JESSICA   When I grow up, I'm gonna be a champion on "Wheel of Fortune" and win millions of dollars in cash and prizes. *(Imitating a contestant)* "I'd like to buy a vowel, Pat. Why Vanna, your dress is just lovely. What? I won again? Oh, it's nothing."

KAREN   Give me a big-time break.

DUKE   OK, OK. Instead of being Elvis, I'll be one of those guys who plays Santa at the mall. *(Stands and begins imitation)* "Ho, ho, ho! Merry Christmas!" *(To friends)* What do you think?

KAREN, JESSICA, NATHAN   *(In unison)* Stick to Elvis.

KAREN	I've got it! *(Stands and pulls Jessica up)* We'll be world-famous models when we get older.
JESSICA	We'll be rich! Hey, I could live with that. *(Karen and Jessica pretend to walk a fashion runway.)*
KAREN	Should we win the Miss America Pageant first?
JESSICA	Definitely.
DUKE	*(Rolling his eyes)* Give it up, ladies. *(They sit.)* Hey, Nathan. What do you wanna be when you grow up?
NATHAN	*(Shrugging his shoulders)* Hey, I'm happy with the way God made me. When I grow up, I just want to be me.
DUKE, JESSICA, KAREN	Oh.
JESSICA	Yeah, well, that's what I meant to say.
KAREN	Yeah. Me, too.
DUKE	Not me. I still want to be Santa. "Ho, ho, ho! Merry Christmas!" *(Nathan, Jessica, and Karen shake their heads and exit.)*
DUKE	Hey, guys! Wait for me! *(He exits.)*

DISCUSSION STARTERS

1. What do you look forward to in the future? What scares you about the future?

2. Read Jeremiah 29:11-13. How does it make you feel to know that God has plans for your future? Why?

3. What dreams do you have for your future? What dreams do you think God has for you?

4. How can we find out and follow God's plans for our future? How can we help others do that?

THE HOMEWORK ZONE

Topic: Schoolwork

by Mike Nappa

The Scene: A classroom.

Characters:

NARRATOR   **STUDENT #1**
SKYLER MITCHELL   **STUDENT #2**
TEACHER

Props: A textbook, a comic book, paper, pencils, "Eerie Music" cue card.

(Before the skit, have the class practice singing an eerie tune like the background music for "The Twilight Zone." During the skit, whenever the narrator flashes the "Eerie Music" cue card, have the audience shout out the tune for five seconds.)

(Skyler is sitting center stage holding a textbook open with a comic book inside it.)

NARRATOR *(With expression, as in an introduction to "The Twilight Zone")* For Skyler Mitchell, this started out like any other study period. *(Skyler does what is described.)* He settled in his chair, opened his world history book, and put the latest "Captain X" comic book inside it to read. But as he drifted to sleep in his chair, he didn't know he was about to enter… The Homework Zone! *(Flashes "Eerie Music" Cue Card.)*

SKYLER *(Drifting off to sleep)* Wow, Captain X sure is cool. Hope there's no test today, though, since I didn't have time to study.

(While Skyler sleeps, Student #1 and Student #2 enter and sit on either side of him. The teacher also enters.)

TEACHER	*(Clearing throat, to Skyler)* Excuse me. *(Skyler snores. Students giggle. Teacher talks louder)* Excuse me!
SKYLER	*(Jumping up)* What? Who? Where? When? How? *(Embarrassed)* Oh, uh, sorry. I must have dozed off. Where am I?
	(Narrator flashes "Eerie Music" cue card.)
TEACHER	In world history class, and it's time for a test. Sit down.
	(Skyler sits. Skyler and students pull out paper and pencils.)
TEACHER	Question #1: How many pink plastic flamingos are sold each year in the United States?
SKYLER	What?
TEACHER	*(Firmly)* You heard the question. Now be quiet and answer it before I take points off your test.
	(Students giggle as they write their answers.)
TEACHER	Question #2: How much does it cost to raise a medium-sized dog to the age of 11?
STUDENT #1	*(Leaning over to whisper to Skyler)* Don't you love it when the questions are right out of the book?
STUDENT #2	*(Leaning over to whisper to Skyler)* Wow, and to think I was worried this might be a tough test.
SKYLER	*(Starting to panic)* What are you guys talking about? I've never heard this stuff before in my life! What's going on here?
	(Narrator flashes "Eerie Music" sign.)
TEACHER	Question #3: True or false. Over two million Americans play the accordion.
	(Students #1 and #2 happily scribble their answers.)
SKYLER	*(Looks back and forth from the students to the teacher and finally explodes)* OK. I admit it! I didn't study! I was reading Captain X!

TEACHER   *(To Skyler)* Answer the questions or you'll have to go back to kindergarten. Question #4: How many telephone-related injuries happen in a year?

SKYLER   Aagghh! *(He runs off stage.)*

TEACHER   *(Shaking head and sighing)* Looks like we lost another one to . . .

NARRATOR   *(Flashes "Eerie Music" cue card)* The Homework Zone.

DISCUSSION STARTERS

1. When have you felt like Skyler? What do you do in those situations?

2. How would following the advice of Colossians 3:17 affect your study habits?

3. What strategies do you use to help you study successfully? How can God help you while you study?

4. Read Ecclesiastes 12:12b. How can you know when it's time to stop studying? What are some positive things you can do for a study break?

THE GETTING-ALONG PATROL

Topic: Getting Along With Others

by Lee Seese

The Scene: Two friends are visited by a stranger during an argument.

Characters:

JESSICA
MELISSA
GETTING-ALONG-PATROL (GAP) AGENT 18

(Tell the audience to make a long buzzer sound that sounds like "Errrr!!!" when GAP Agent 18 raises his or her hand.)

JESSICA	And another thing, I don't care if you are my best friend. I'll call you whatever I want to.
MELISSA	Just because I told you your hair looks dumb doesn't mean you have to kill me with some bad name.
JESSICA	Well, my hair might look dumb, but at least I wash it once in a while.
MELISSA	Maybe you should wash your mouth out sometime.
JESSICA	Maybe I should smack your mouth, Munchkin Melissa.
MELISSA	Well, maybe I . . .
GAP	*(enters quickly)* OK, girls, hold it right there.
JESSICA	Hey, who are you?
MELISSA	Where did you come from?
GAP	Agent 18. I'm with the GAP.

JESSICA	The GAP?
GAP	The Getting-Along Patrol. We promote pals peacefully, patiently, practicing polite partnership without pounding people or pouting.
MELISSA	Pretty powerful!
JESSICA	Puh—leaz! So what do you want with us?
GAP	We want to promote pals peacefully, patiently, practicing polite partnership without pounding people or pouting.
JESSICA	I think you already said that, GAP Sap!
MELISSA	You're funny, Jess.
GAP	That's a matter of opinion. You aren't getting along with others when you say something that hurts.
JESSICA	But what if it makes people laugh?
GAP	Making someone laugh on the outside could mean someone crying on the inside.
JESSICA	Melissa cries on the outside, like a baby.
MELISSA	At least I don't suck my thumb.
GAP	*(Raises hand to signal audience to make the buzzer sound.)* Errr!!!
JESSICA	Wow! What was that?
GAP	That was the GAP Snap-Out-of-It Buzzer. If you even start to say or do anything that doesn't promote pals peacefully, patiently, practicing polite partnership without pounding people or pouting, you will hear that sound.
JESSICA	What a stupid . . .
GAP, AUDIENCE	Errr!!!
MELISSA	Of all the idio . . .

GAP, AUDIENCE	Errr!!! I can see you girls will be a real project.
JESSICA	You're right, I guess. But we can use the help. Right, Missy?
MELISSA	I'll say! We should get along better so we don't hurt each other.
JESSICA	Yeah, and we should give GAP Agent 18 a break. He looks like he could use a vacation.

DISCUSSION STARTERS

1. Why is it hard to get along with others? Who do you have the hardest time getting along with? Why?

2. How busy would the Getting Along Patrol be if they dropped in on you? Would it help you if there really was a GAP? Since there is no such thing, what can you do to try to get along with others better?

3. How many things can you think of that will help you get along with others? Read Colossians 3:12-17 for some ideas.

A Pack of Bologna

Topic: Parents

by Lee Seese

The Scene: A boy, who is angry with his parents, advises a friend who is running away from home.

Characters:

DAD
JOSH
JUSTIN

DAD	*(Makes this jibberish sound like the adults in "Peanuts" cartoons)* Mwa, mwa, mwa!
JOSH	OK, OK, I'm coming, Dad. Do you think I'm deaf or something?
DAD	Mwa, mwa, mwa, wmp, mwa.
JOSH	Why do *I* always have to take out the garbage?
DAD	Mwa, mwa, mwaup, mwaup, mwa.
JOSH	Well, every Tuesday *seems* like always. Can't I do it after I watch TV?
DAD	Mwa.
JOSH	You're so unfair! *(Picks up garbage and slams door. He spots Justin walking down the road carrying a paper bag.)*
JUSTIN	*(Calling)* Hi, Josh!
JOSH	Hey, Justin. What are you doing?
JUSTIN	Running away.

JOSH	From home?
JUSTIN	No, from a herd of buffaloes.
JOSH	Why?
JUSTIN	They're bigger than me!
JOSH	Come on! What happened?
JUSTIN	First of all, my mom won't let me watch TV until I do my homework.
JOSH	Sounds like my mom!
JUSTIN	But the worst thing is that I gotta clean my room every Saturday.
JOSH	What do you use? A shovel?
JUSTIN	Very funny. It's not *that* messy. I'm just sick of always obeying my parents.
JOSH	I know what you mean. They think they're in charge or something. Hey, what's in the bag?
JUSTIN	Supplies.
JOSH	Like what?
JUSTIN	Stuff to survive on 'til I get there. You know—licorice, a pack of bologna, and clean underwear.
JOSH	Underwear?
JUSTIN	My mom always says I should have clean underwear in case I have to go to the hospital.
JOSH	Oh, yeah! Where are you running away to?
JUSTIN	Canada.
JOSH	Canada?
JUSTIN	Matt Dello says they don't have to obey their parents up there.

JOSH	Matt also says his dad flew to Mars one time.
DAD	Mwa, mwa, mwaa, mwap.
JOSH	OK, Dad. Can Justin eat with us tonight?
DAD	Mwa.
JOSH	Thanks, Dad. Come on, Justin. My dad is pretty smart. Maybe he can take you to Canada . . . or back home!

DISCUSSION STARTERS

1. Read Ephesians 6:1-4. What do you find in that passage that surprises you? What's the best thing to do when you're frustrated with your parents?

2. If there really were a country where kids didn't have to obey their parents, what would it be like? Would you want to live there?

3. Read Colossians 3:20. Why do you think God is pleased when you obey your parents? When is it hardest to obey your parents? What can you do to make it easier?

The Prayer Pair

Topic: Talking to God

by Lee Seese

The Scene: A Sunday school teacher has just finished a lesson on prayer. She's asked students to pray in pairs together before they leave.

Characters:

RHONDA *(Very sincere, she's learned a lot about prayer. Her hands are folded and her eyes are tightly closed.)*

BRIAN *(Easily distracted, he occasionally peeks, yawns, and forgets who he's talking to.)*

RHONDA   Dear God.

BRIAN   Who can give us lots of stuff.

RHONDA   Thank you for loving us.

BRIAN   Even when we don't pay attention in class.

RHONDA   Forgive our sins.

BRIAN   Especially my little sister who, I guess you know, is really a brat.

RHONDA   Thank you for being so kind.

BRIAN   Hey! Maybe you could do a miracle and make Mrs. Mickle kind. *(Looks up as if looking at the teacher and shakes head. Then quickly bows head.)*

RHONDA   God, I ask that you give strength and safety to our missionaries.

BRIAN   Yeah, and why don't you give 'em some cool clothes to wear for a change, too. And while you are at it, I could use some new tennis shoes.

RHONDA   *(Claps her hand over his Brian's mouth)* Sorry, God. Where was I?

BRIAN   In the Sunday school room, silly.

(Rhonda glares at Brian.)

RHONDA   Thank you for giving us food.

BRIAN   Except broccoli.

RHONDA   And a place to live.

BRIAN   Jimmy Dunlap has a pool at his house. Give me each day a daily dip in my own pool.

RHONDA   Lead us not into temptation but deliver us from evil.

BRIAN   Deliver us a pizza after church so I don't have to eat Mom's lumpy smashed potatoes.

RHONDA   Help us to do our best in school.

BRIAN   And be bountifully generous when report cards come.

RHONDA   *(Looks to him and whispers)* Bountifully generous?

BRIAN   *(Defensively)* The minister says that sometimes.

RHONDA   Oh, and help our minister as he preaches this morning.

BRIAN   Yes, may his watch be 15 minutes fast.

RHONDA   May Brian and I pay attention.

BRIAN   Like I always do.

RHONDA   And help me put up with Brian. Amen!

BRIAN   Amen!! It's about time! What did you want to do, Rhonda—put God to sleep?

DISCUSSION STARTERS

1. When you pray, are you more like Rhonda or Brian? What do you usually pray about? Why is talking to God important?

2. Read Daniel 6:6-23. What can we learn about prayer from these verses?

3. What would you do if it were against the law to pray to God?

As We Say and Do

Topic: Peer Pressure

by Julianne Bruce

THE SCENE: Two girls are trying to convince their friend to do the "in" thing.

CHARACTERS:

CHRISTINE
NOELLE
WENDY

(This skit could also be played by three boys.)

WENDY	Come on, why won't you do it? Everyone else is doing it.
NOELLE	Yeah. You're just about the only one who isn't.
CHRISTINE	But I'm just not sure.
NOELLE	What's there to be sure about? Just go for it. It's no big deal.
CHRISTINE	I guess I just feel weird about it.
WENDY	I know. I didn't really want to do it at first either. But once you do it, it's easy.
CHRISTINE	Really?
WENDY	Would I lie? Look, if you do it, everyone will think you're cool. If you don't ...
NOELLE	I'm not sure I want to be friends with someone who isn't doing it. I mean, everybody knows.
CHRISTINE	You'd dump me just because of *this?*

WENDY   It's simple. Yes or no?

CHRISTINE   All right. If it's that big a deal, I guess I'll do it.

WENDY   I knew you would!

NOELLE   Here. *(Reaches into a paper sack and pulls out three plastic buckets. Each girl puts one on her head.)*

WENDY   Now you're cool.

NOELLE   I can't believe you almost didn't do it. *(She and Wendy exit.)*

CHRISTINE   *(Gives audience a shrug and sighs)* Great. *(She exits.)*

DISCUSSION STARTERS

1. What kinds of things do you feel pressured by your friends to do ?

2. How does it make you feel when you give into something just to go along with the crowd?

3. What happens to people who always do what everyone else seems to be doing?

4. Read 1 Kings 18:20-39. How was Elijah rewarded for not following the crowd?

BOREDOM BLUES

Topic: Entertainment
by Julianne Bruce

The Scene: Three boys are doing the same old thing for fun, and three girls are doing something fun and creative.

Characters:

CHRIS (Nikki's brother) **NIKKI** (Chris' sister)
DEAN (Chris' friend) **TONIA** (Nikki's friend)
SHAWN (Chris' friend) **HOLLY** (Nikki's friend)

(The boys are sitting on one side of the room watching TV. Behind them, in the kitchen, the girls are baking. The girls should laugh a lot and make it sound like fun.)

CHRIS   This movie is so boring.

DEAN   It'd help if we hadn't already seen it.

SHAWN   Nothing else was on. You want to watch videos?

CHRIS   No, we did that all day. How about some computer games? *(Looks over his shoulder to see what's going on in the kitchen.)*

SHAWN   What are they doing?

CHRIS   I don't know.

DEAN   Sure sounds like more fun than this.

SHAWN   Let's go find out. *(The boys get up and go to the kitchen.)*

CHRIS   Hey, Sis, whatcha doing?

NIKKI   We're baking, why?

CHRIS	No reason. You're sure making a lot of noise.
TONIA	That's because we're having so much fun.
NIKKI	What're you guys doing?
DEAN	Nothing.
CHRIS	We were so. We were watching a movie.
SHAWN	Like he said, nothing.
DEAN	What are you baking?
HOLLY	*(With pride)* Chocolate cake—from scratch.
SHAWN	Sounds like it takes a long time.
TONIA	Not that long. Besides, it's fun.
DEAN	Do you guys do this every weekend?
HOLLY	No way. That'd be boring. We think up lots of other things to do.
CHRIS	Like what?
NIKKI	Well, we sure don't watch movies and videos all day. We make up interesting stuff, like different kinds of parties.
DEAN	What kind of parties?
TONIA	You know, different themes and stuff.
NIKKI	And once we had a sleepover and stayed up all night making a radio show. We played our CD's and took turns being the deejay.
DEAN	You guys do all sorts of cool stuff.
SHAWN	Yeah. And we always do the same old boring stuff.
TONIA	You just have to be creative. But then, maybe guys aren't as creative as girls.
CHRIS	We are, too! We can come up with all sorts of cool things to do.

NIKKI	Like what?
DEAN	*(Pausing to think)* Like helping you bake a cake.
SHAWN	And helping you eat it! *(Tries to smear one of the girls with frosting. Everyone joins in.)*

DISCUSSION STARTERS

1. What kinds of creative things do you do for fun? What other kinds of things can you think of that would be fun to try?

2. Read Ephesians 5:15-20. What does the Bible say about how we should spend our time? Is it wrong just to have fun sometimes?

It's Up to You

Topic: Making Decisions

by Julianne Bruce

The Scene: A courtroom. There's a chair in the middle of the room where the decision maker sits and a chair set back and off to one side for the judge. The lawyers stand on either side and pace in front of the audience.

Characters:

SALLY, THE DECISION MAKER   **LAWYER #1**
THE JUDGE   **LAWYER #2**

(Note: The roles in this scene can be played by either girls or boys.)

JUDGE *(Addressing the audience as the jury)* Ladies and gentlemen of the jury, you have before you today a girl with a decision to make. Her parents have left this decision entirely up to her, and she must make her choice today. The lawyers will present their evidence, and you must help her decide what to do. Lawyer #1, you may proceed.

LAWYER #1 Sally, is it true that you have to choose between going to basketball camp and earning money by taking care of your neighbor's house while they're on vacation?

SALLY Yes.

LAWYER #1 Why can't you do both?

SALLY My neighbors are going out of town the same two weeks as camp.

LAWYER #1 Isn't it obvious to you, Sally, that learning to improve your basketball skills is far more important than making a little bit of money?

SALLY   Well, the money could help me buy new high-tops for next season.

LAWYER #2   And aren't new shoes really more important, Sally? How are you going to play basketball in your old, worn-out shoes?

SALLY   I guess I could try to get some other kind of job this summer after camp.

LAWYER #2   But there's no guarantee, is there? You might not be able to find any more work. Then where will you be?

SALLY   I guess I . . .

LAWYER #1   *(Interrupting)* But, Sally, if you don't go to camp and improve your skills, you might not even make the team. Then what's the point of getting new shoes?

SALLY   It might . . .

LAWYER #2   *(Interrupting)* Isn't helping out your neighbors more important than going to camp? You can always practice on your own.

LAWYER #1   Couldn't you make a lot of new friends at camp? Those friendships could really mean a lot to you next year at school.

LAWYER #2   Come on, Sally, you know what to do.

LAWYER #1   Sure you do, just tell him that you want to go to camp.

SALLY   But I don't know! That's the problem. Both things are good. What am I supposed to do? I can't decide!

JUDGE   Ladies and gentlemen of the jury, it is now time for you to do your job. Which is it going to be? All in favor of basketball camp, raise your hand. *(Count the hands.)* All in favor of working for the neighbors, raise your hand. *(Count the hands.)* Well, Sally, it looks like the decision has been made for you. You are going to . . . *(Repeat whichever decision got the most votes.)* You may step down.

SALLY   OK, but I'm still not sure.

DISCUSSION STARTERS

1. Why is it sometimes so hard to make a decision?

2. How do you usually go about making a decision when a choice has been left up to you?

3. Tell about a bad decision you made and what you learned from it.

4. Read Psalm 73:24. How does it feel to know that God will guide you? Tell about a time when you knew that God was guiding you.

THE MONEYMAKERS

Topic: Trust

by Julianne Bruce

The Scene: Two brothers are trying to decide how to earn money.

Characters:

MARK
SCOTT

MARK	I don't get it. We need to make some money, but nobody will give us a job.
SCOTT	It's not fair! Mom and Dad always say we're supposed to be responsible. How can we be responsible when nobody wants to give us a chance?
MARK	Yeah. Like I asked Mrs. Wilson if I could give her poodle a bath again, and she shut the door in my face. I thought Fluffy looked pretty good last time. I even gave him a haircut, remember?
SCOTT	Well...it was kind of more like a mohawk. He was bald for a month!
MARK	It wasn't bad for my first try. *(Pauses to think.)* Hey, did you ask Mom if we could mow the lawn?
SCOTT	She said no. I don't know why. Last time we mowed every single bit. We didn't miss a spot.
MARK	I guess we probably shouldn't have run over the tulips, though.
SCOTT	It was an accident. *(Pauses to think.)* Maybe Dad would let us paint the garage! We did it really fast last summer.

MARK   We better not ask. I think he's still kind of mad that we painted over the windows.

SCOTT   I wish we still had our newspaper route. That would make us a bunch of money.

MARK   I don't see why we got fired. We delivered every single paper.

SCOTT   I guess it would have been better if we hadn't delivered them all to one house.

MARK   So what are we going to do for money?

SCOTT   I just don't know. It's like nobody trusts us. I don't understand it.

MARK   Me neither. Hey, I've got an idea! Why don't we chop some wood and sell it to people?

SCOTT   Great idea! *(Boys start to exit.)* Doesn't Mr. Jackson have a big oak tree in his yard? We could get a lot of wood from that!

(Boys exit.)

DISCUSSION STARTERS

1. Tell about a time when you thought someone should trust you, but they didn't.

2. How do you know who *you* can trust?

3. Read Romans 8:28. Do you ever find it hard to trust God? Explain.

4. Read Matthew 14:22-33. Do you think Peter was wrong for not trusting Jesus? Would you have been able to trust Jesus in the same situation?

LIFE 101

Topic: Being Liked by Others

by Rich Melheim

The Scene: Four guest speakers talk to a college class about how to get people to like you.

Characters:

PROFESSOR   GUEST #3

GUEST #1   GUEST #4

GUEST #2

PROFESSOR *(Yelling)* Attention! Attention! Thank you. I just love attention. Welcome, ladies and gentlemen, to your first day in college. This class is titled "How to Get People to Like You." For the first session, I've invited a panel of guests to share their views. Guest #1 . . .

GUEST #1 To get people to like you, you must first tell them how great you are. Everyone, repeat after me: "I am the greatest! I am the greatest!" *(Trying to get the audience to say this)* Come on! "I am the greatest! I am the greatest!"

GUEST #2 No, no, no. That doesn't do any good. In order to really get people to like you, you've got to wear the right kind of clothes and be up on the latest styles. For instance, did you know that the "in" crowd is wearing their shoes on their hands this season? Yes! Everyone, now please do exactly as I do. *(She tries to get everyone to put their shoes on their hands. Guest #1 attempts to keep the crowd shouting, "I am the greatest.")* Come on! Get with it!

GUEST #3 No, no, no, no, no. In order to truly be liked by others, you've got to have a beautiful body. You've got to be in shape. Muscle tone—that's the ticket. Everyone, do exactly what I do. First, jumping jacks. One, two, three . . . come on.

Now, sit-ups. One, two, three... (*Guests #1 and #2 continue to coax group to do as they wish.*)

GUEST #4   No, no, no, no, no, no, no! You're all wet. Every one of you. In order to get others to like you, you've got to do the right kind of drugs. Drugs! That's what I said. And did you know that it is a scientific fact that certain kinds of shoe leather, when combined with foot odor, produce a great high? Yes! Everyone, take off your shoes. Come on. Start to sniff. There you go! (*Other guests continue to try to coax the crowd to follow them, louder, louder, and louder.*) Come on. Sniff!

PROFESSOR   (*Yelling at top of lungs*) Waaait! Can't they just be themselves? Why do they have to do all this stupid stuff? God made them who they are, and that's just fine! If their friends don't like them for who they are, then maybe there's something wrong with their friends!

GUEST #1   (*Long pause*) Be themselves?

GUEST #2   What a strange idea.

GUEST #3   Do you think it'll work?

GUEST #4   If it doesn't, they can always try sniffing a shoe.

PROFESSOR   Lovely. Class dismissed! (*Walking away, shaking his head.*)

DISCUSSION STARTERS

1. Why is being popular so important to some people?

2. Think of one time when someone you know did something wrong just to be accepted. What happened?

3. Describe a time in your life when you felt like you didn't belong.

4. Read John 15:18-25. What does this say about being liked by others? When is it wrong to work at being liked by others?

THE DIVORCE DUMPS

Topic: Divorce

by Sue Norris Janetzke

The Scene: In Barb's family's kitchen, Angie receives help concerning her parents' separation and divorce.

Characters:

ANGIE
BARB

Props: Books, table, and chairs

(Angie and Barb walk into Barb's family's kitchen. It's after school, and they're going to study together.)

BARB   Whew—I'm glad this school day is finally over! Would you like something to drink before we start on that science homework?

ANGIE   No thanks. I guess I'd rather get to work and get it over with.

BARB   All right. *(They put their books on the table and sit down.)* How should we begin?

ANGIE   I don't care. Whatever you think is fine.

BARB   Well, how about starting it out with an experiment? We could blow something up and then explain it to the class in our report.

ANGIE   That sounds fine. Just tell me what to do, and I'll do it.

BARB   Angie, before we start on this, I need some help from you. I just can't face this all by myself.

     (Angie puts her head down and sobs.)

BARB   Gee, Angie, I'll help. What's wrong?

ANGIE   *(Sobbing)* Everybody wants something from me. I can't do anything right. It seems as if no one even cares. I can't take it anymore.

BARB   What are you talking about, Angie? You can talk to me. I won't tell anyone what you say, honest.

ANGIE   My folks split up. All they've done for the last year is yell and argue with each other. And now that they're getting a divorce, all they do is yell at my brother Tom and me. Things cost too much, we like one of them better than the other one—stuff like that.

BARB   I'm sorry about your parents, Angie. But the divorce isn't your fault.

ANGIE   Sure. Tell my folks that. It feels like they really don't love either one of us!

BARB   I'm sure that they love you both.

ANGIE   All they care about is who gets the car, the house, and the couch. They're only fighting over us because they think we're property, too, and they don't want the other person to get more than they get. I feel like a piece of furniture.

BARB   You must know that deep down inside, your parents are angry at each other. They still love you.

ANGIE   I guess, but they have a funny way of showing it. I feel like my whole world is coming apart. Nothing is ever going to be the same again.

DISCUSSION STARTERS

1. Why does divorce hurt so much?

2. Read Romans 8:31-39. What encouragement could you share with Angie?

3. If your friend's family were going through a divorce, what could you do to help your friend?

Your Secret's Safe With Me

Topic: Gossip

by Sue Norris Janetzke

The Scene: On the playground at lunch, students discuss the weekend.

Characters:

ALICE   CATHY
SALLY   DENISE
MARY

ALICE   Hi, Sally. What's happening? Have a good weekend? Can you keep a secret?

SALLY   No problem.

ALICE   You will never believe what I saw happen this weekend! About 8 o'clock Friday night, I saw an ambulance and a police car at Mary's house!

SALLY   No kidding! What happened?

ALICE   I'm not exactly sure, but Mary's brother used to get into trouble a lot. I bet it had something to do with him. Word around the neighborhood is that someone broke into a neighbor's garage.

SALLY   Wow! Well, I gotta go.

     (Alice exits. As Sally walks away, she pulls Cathy off to the side and whispers.)

SALLY   Hey, Cathy, can you keep a secret?

CATHY	Sure.
SALLY	Did you hear about what happened to Mary's brother?
CATHY	No. What?
SALLY	I heard he may have broken into someone's house! The police came to his house and everything. There was an ambulance there, too.
CATHY	When did this happen?
SALLY	Friday night, really late.
CATHY	Wow! I bet Mary's embarrassed. It would be terrible to have a thief for a brother. What was the ambulance for?
SALLY	I don't know. Someone must have gotten hurt.
CATHY	What a shame! See ya.

(Sally exits. As Cathy walks away, she pulls Denise off to the side and whispers.)

CATHY	Denise, did you hear about Mary's brother being arrested by the police?
DENISE	No, I haven't heard a thing.
CATHY	It seems that he broke into some rich person's house. I heard he may have gotten shot because there was an ambulance at his house, real late at night. Last night, I think.

(Just then, the bell rings to go in from recess. All speakers to their seats. Mary stands in front of the class to talk.)

MARY	I asked our teacher if I could talk to the class. I know that there are stories going around about me. I want to tell everyone what really happened. Friday night, the police and an ambulance came to our house. Our next-door neighbor, Mr. McDougherity, had come over to borrow one of our dad's power tools. All of a sudden, he held his chest and fell to the floor right on our front porch. He acted as if he couldn't breathe. John and I were home alone, so I called 911 and got a blanket while John start-ed CPR. A police car was in the area when the call went in, and he arrived first and took over the CPR for John. The paramedics

said our quick thinking and John's CPR training may have saved Mr. McDougherity's life. We found out later that he had a slight heart attack. We might even get on the news because we helped him. It was really exciting!

DISCUSSION STARTERS

1. What is gossip? What could the girls have done to keep the gossip from spreading?

2. Tell about a time when gossip hurt someone you know. Why is it so tempting to pass along gossip?

3. Read Proverbs 16:28 and James 1:26. What do these verses teach us about how Christians should react to gossip? What do you need to do when you think about what to talk about?

THE BIG DAY

Topic: God's Promises

by Brian Mason

The Scene: It's the day of the big vacation Bible school presentation, and it's raining.

Characters:

LEAH
GREGG
BRIAN

LEAH	I can't believe it's raining.
GREGG	I guess we'll just have to call off the presentation.
LEAH	And we worked so hard making the stage look like Noah's ark!
BRIAN	Cheer up, you two. We've got signs posted everywhere...the playground, the school, and all of the stores. I'm sure we'll have at least two kids from every street here!
GREGG	Get real, Brian. The only ones who'll show up in this weather are ducks.
BRIAN	Aren't you forgetting something?
LEAH	Yeah, our umbrellas.
GREGG	And our boots!
BRIAN	Not!! You're forgetting God's promise that the world would not be destroyed by waters again.
LEAH	Time for a reality check, Brian. The program starts in 40 minutes, not 40 days.

BRIAN   True, but God kept his promise then, and he'll keep his promise today. Don't you think God wants us to do this presentation to get the neighborhood excited about vacation Bible school?

GREGG   But everyone will be laughing at us singing in the rain!

BRIAN   Didn't they laugh at Noah?

LEAH   Yeah, I guess you're right. Let's start getting things set up.

(Everyone pretends to set up chairs and decorations for the program.)

BRIAN   Hey, is it my imagination or is the rain starting to let up?

GREGG   This is unreal...here comes the sun!

LEAH   Wow!...Look! There's a rainbow over the stage.

GREGG   And here come the kids!

BRIAN   God *always* keeps his promises...yesterday, today, and tomorrow!

(Kids give one another high fives!)

DISCUSSION STARTERS

1. Tell about a time you know God kept a promise to you. Did the situation work out the way you expected it to? Explain.

2. Read Genesis 8:20-22. How is this skit similar to the story of Noah's ark? How does God's promise to Noah affect our future?

3. Read Psalm 145:13 and John 15:17. If God always keeps promises, why don't our prayers always get answered the way we expect them to be?

4. How does it make you feel to know that God always keeps his promises? What has God promised to do for you?

A Smile and a Song

Topic: Joyful Living

by Brian Mason

The Scene: Two guys chat at their lockers at the end of a school day on a Friday afternoon.

Characters:

JAKE
NICK

(Jake is humming a praise song as the skit begins.)

NICK	I wish you'd chill out. People are starting to talk!
JAKE	Talk about what?
NICK	Talk about you. You're always humming or you've got a silly grin on your face.
JAKE	I do?
NICK	Yeah! And you go right up and start talking to anybody, like they're your long-lost brother or something. How embarrassing!
JAKE	Then why do you keep hanging around?
NICK	Well, you are kind of weird...I mean different...but you aren't that way just to get attention.
JAKE	Sounds like you're curious.
NICK	Well, I am. I mean you're not rich, you're not brilliant, and you're definitely not a super jock!
JAKE	You forgot to add that the girls don't think I'm cute.

NICK	That, too! But for some reason, they all want your school picture, and they like talking to you.
JAKE	Maybe money, brains, sports, and looks aren't what makes someone happy.
NICK	OK, then what's your secret?
JAKE	Do you really want to know?
NICK	Sure I do!
JAKE	Then come to my party tonight.
NICK	I didn't think you were the partying type.
JAKE	Oh, this isn't just some ol' party—it's a huge celebration. There'll be singing and dancing. We'll probably have so much fun and laugh so hard our stomachs will hurt for a week.
NICK	Sounds radical. What's the occasion?
JAKE	We've got a special guest.
NICK	Anyone I know?
JAKE	Not yet, but I'm hoping you will soon!
NICK	What's so special about this guy?
JAKE	Well, first of all, he loves everybody. And second, he's more fun than anyone I know.
NICK	Wow! This sounds kinda fun.
JAKE	There is only one way to find out for sure.
NICK	OK, OK, I'll come. What time?
JAKE	You can come any time you want. He's at my house all the time.

(Jake starts humming again, shuts his locker, and exits. Nick looks at him with a puzzled expression.)

DISCUSSION STARTERS

1. Why do you think Nick keeps hanging around Jake? What can we learn from Jake?

2. Read John 15:1-11. What's the secret of having joy in your life? Describe the kind of joy a Christian has.

3. Create an ending to this story by telling what might happen at the party that night.

REPORT CARDS

Topic: School Performance

The Scene: Two classmates walking home from school after getting their report cards.

Characters:

SAMANTHA
BRENDA

SAMANTHA   Hey, Brenda, wait up! What's your hurry?

BRENDA   I hate school, I hate grades, and I hate Straight-A Jenny Cooper!

SAMANTHA   Uh-oh! What did you get on your report card?

BRENDA   Four A's and three B's.

SAMANTHA   Wow, that's super! I got four C's and three B's.

BRENDA   Then you must really be bummed out!

SAMANTHA   Not really...I learned a lot this semester, and my parents are really happy.

BRENDA   How can they be happy? They haven't even seen your report card yet!

SAMANTHA   No, but they mailed my letter.

BRENDA   Mailed your letter? I don't get it.

SAMANTHA   Well, in English class we learned how to structure and write a letter. So I wrote the family Christmas letter.

BRENDA   I don't remember that homework assignment.

SAMANTHA   It wasn't homework, silly! I wanted to do it. My dad always says that people don't care how much you know, until they know how much you care. My parents were both really busy, so I helped out some.

BRENDA That saying of your dad's sounds like something from the Bible.

SAMANTHA Actually, it sounds like Jesus. He knew everything and still took time to share and to care for others in a way they could understand. *(Pause.)* Sort of like you!

BRENDA Like me? What do you mean?

SAMANTHA Like when you skipped Jenny's big skating and pizza party to tutor me for the math test on money.

BRENDA But I wasn't that great a tutor. You didn't even get an A on the test.

SAMANTHA No, but I learned enough to save up some money and to buy this for you!

BRENDA What is it? *(Pretends to open a small gift)* Oh, it's so pretty!

SAMANTHA Read it!

BRENDA *(Pretends to read a plaque)* "Wisdom and understanding are a treasure from God." It's beautiful. I guess I do put too much emphasis on grades.

SAMANTHA Good grades are important, Brenda. But Jesus told us that it's more important to help others and to use what we know to help the kingdom of God.

BRENDA I guess that means I can't hate Straight-A Jenny, huh?

SAMANTHA Right! Plus, straight A's won't get you into heaven anyway! *(Pause.)* You know, we really ought to invite Jenny to our church group.

BRENDA Yeah, you're right... with all that brain power, she just might have some creative ideas for our group!

SAMANTHA Now that's the smartest thing you've said all day!

(They both laugh.)

DISCUSSION STARTERS

1. Do you feel pressured to get good grades? Why?

2. Are you more like Brenda or Samantha? Explain.

3. Read Proverbs 2:1-10. Explain what wisdom is.

4. Read Colossians 3:23. How does this verse apply to schoolwork? Do you think getting good grades should always be top priority? Why or why not?

More Practical Resources for Your Children's Ministry

Children's Ministry Magazine's Best-Ever Ideas

The greatest games...craftiest crafts...and spectacular seasonal activities that make *every* day feel like a holiday—collected and ready for your class! You'll never be stuck again for a fun idea to liven up your classroom! Just flip through this compilation of the very best ideas to appear in Children's Ministry Magazine for...

- Role plays...
- Cooperative games...
- Lively, singable songs...
- Dynamic devotions...
- Praise and worship...
- Creative crafts...
- Edible art...and
- Small-group activities.

Plus, the handy index will help you choose just the right activity for *your* kids, from nursery straight up through elementary school!
1-55945-623-X

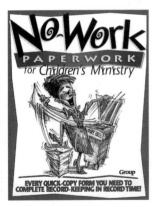

No-Work Paperwork for Children's Ministry

Take the headache out of planning...prep time...and administration with over 100 easy-to-use, quick-copy forms you'll *never* need to write again for...

- Recruiting volunteers...
- Tracking expenses...
- Getting parents' permissions...
- Organizing events...and
- Staying on top of calendars, checklists, requests, and reminders.

Use these fast forms to stay organized...keep tabs on your budget...and cover legal requirements that come with children's ministry. Plus, you'll have more time to work with kids!
1-55945-621-3

Use Your Overhead Projector to Transport Your Children Into Colorful, Life-Size Bible Scenes...

Big Action Bible Skits

Here's drama that's exciting and easy! Eight Full-color overhead transparencies and 5- to 10-minute skits let children act our favorite Old Testament stories—without expensive scenery and props! Simply shine an overhead on a blank wall and presto—instant staging!

Skits and overheads include...
•Adam and Eve,
•Noah and the Ark,
•Moses and the Exodus,
•Jonah, and other favorites you'll use again and again!

Perfect for Sunday school, Christian day school, children's worship, or anywhere you want your children to learn Bible stories—and have fun at the same time!
1-55945-258-7

Group's Singable Songs for Children's Ministry

62 of the best sing-along songs for your children's ministry, including...
- **Classics,** such as "Wise Man and the Foolish Man" and "The Butterfly Song"
- **Contemporary** children's songs, such as "The Holy Books" by James Ward and "Hip Hip Hooray" by Mary Rice Hopkins
- **Brand new** favorites—"Sing If You Wanna Be Happy" by Caye Cook, "The Family" by Barry McGuire and Mark Royce, and others!

Accompaniment & Leaders Guide

Included are complete piano scores and guitar chords for 62 favorites. Also tips for making simple instruments children can create and play, and ideas for turning singing into a learning opportunity! Keep little fingers busy with hand motions for over 30 songs and sign-language instructions for over a dozen songs!
1-55945-464-4

Lyrics Big Book for Group Singing

Illustrated to help kids learn and sing songs! Includes "Hip Hip Hooray," "It's a Miracle," and 13 more!
1-55945-465-2

Lyrics Big Book for More Group Singing

Illustrated, includes "You're Something Special," "Let Everybody Praise the Lord," and 13 more!
1-55945-466-0

Split-Channel Compact Discs and Cassettes

The handy split-channel format lets you play both music and vocals while your children learn songs—and just the music once you've mastered them!

Volume 1	Cassette 1-55945-455-5	Compact Disc 1-55945-459-8
Volume 2	Cassette 1-55945-456-3	Compact Disc 1-55945-460-1
Volume 3	Cassette 1-55945-457-1	Compact Disc 1-55945-461-X
Volume 4	Cassette 1-55945-458-X	Compact Disc 1-55945-462-8

Order today from your local Christian bookstore, or write: Group Publishing, Box 485, Loveland, CO 80539.

BRING THE BIBLE TO LIFE FOR YOUR 1ST THROUGH 6TH GRADERS WITH GROUP'S HANDS-ON BIBLE CURRICULUM™

Energize your kids with Active Learning!

Group's **Hands-On Bible Curriculum**™ will help you teach the Bible in a radical new way. It's based on Active Learning—the same teaching method Jesus used.

In each lesson, students will participate in exciting and memorable learning experiences using fascinating gadgets and gizmos you've not seen with any other curriculum. Your elementary students will discover biblical truths and <u>remember</u> what they learn because they're <u>doing</u> instead of just listening.

You'll save time and money too!

While students are learning more, you'll be working less—simply follow the quick and easy instructions in the **Teachers Guide**. You'll get tons of material for an energy-packed 35- to 60-minute lesson. In addition to the easy-to-use **Teachers Guide**, you'll get all the essential teaching materials you need in a ready-to-use **Learning Lab**®. Plus, you'll SAVE BIG over other curriculum programs that require you to buy expensive separate student books—all student handouts in Group's **Hands-On Bible Curriculum** are photocopiable!

Challenging topics each quarter keep your kids coming back!

Group's **Hands-On Bible Curriculum** covers topics that matter to your kids and teaches them the Bible with integrity. Switching topics every month keeps your 1st- through 6th-graders enthused and coming back for more. The full two-year program will help your kids...
- make God-pleasing decisions,
- recognize their God-given potential, and
- seek to grow as Christians.

Take the boredom out of Sunday school, children's church, and youth group for your elementary students. Make your job easier and more rewarding with no-fail lessons that are ready in a flash. Order Group's **Hands-On Bible Curriculum** for your 1st- through 6th-graders today.

Hands-On Bible Curriculum is also available for Toddlers & 2s, Preschool, and Pre-K and K!

Order today from your local Christian bookstore, or write: Group Publishing, Box 485, Loveland, CO 80539.